Original title:
What I Learned

Copyright © 2024 Swan Charm
All rights reserved.

Author: Liina Liblikas
ISBN HARDBACK: 978-9916-79-182-0
ISBN PAPERBACK: 978-9916-79-183-7
ISBN EBOOK: 978-9916-79-184-4

Dialogues with the Infinite

In quiet chambers of the heart,
Where whispers dance with sacred air,
I seek the voice that will impart,
The truths beyond our earthly care.

The stars above, a canvas bright,
Paint words of hope in endless night,
Each twinkle, like a sacred part,
Of conversations that we start.

In prayer, a bridge is gently drawn,
Connecting me to realms unknown,
Where mercy flows like early dawn,
And love is endlessly sown.

The shadows fade, the spirit soars,
To realms where faith forever stands,
In silence, I hear distant roars,
Of angels mingling in hushed bands.

With every breath, I find the grace,
To see the hand that guides my way,
In dialogues with the infinite,
I am reborn with each new day.

Beneath the Light of Faith

Beneath the light, the shadows flee,
A warmth that fills the fractured soul,
In faith, we find our destiny,
A compass guiding towards the whole.

The heart, a vessel filled with dreams,
Awaits the dawn's illuminating touch,
In every prayer, each silence seems,
To echo love, embrace us much.

With every dawn, a chance to rise,
To share the burden, heal the pain,
In unity, the spirit flies,
Inviting hope to reign again.

The trials faced like passing storms,
Will lead us to the sacred shore,
Where souls connect in myriad forms,
And doubt becomes a distant roar.

Beneath the sky, where mercy reigns,
We stand as one, our voices blend,
In light of faith, the world regains,
The peace that grows as we ascend.

Eternal Echoes in a Temporal World

In moments fleeting, echoes call,
Whispers of ages, deep and wide,
Each heartbeat tells a sacred thrall,
Of journeys shared, where love abides.

Time flows like rivers, swift and sure,
Yet in each wave, a truth remains,
Eternal echoes, pure and pure,
Retelling tales of joy and pains.

Through trials faced and paths we tread,
The spirit shines, a constant light,
In every tear and word unsaid,
We find the strength to bear our plight.

Thus anchored by the stars above,
We reach for hands that guide us through,
In every heartbeat, bleeds the love,
That time cannot erase anew.

In this temporal world we dwell,
Eternal whispers stir the soul,
In fleeting moments, magic swells,
To teach us all we are made whole.

The Path of Sacred Understanding

In quiet moments, truth unfolds,
Whispers of wisdom, gently told.
Hearts gather light, as shadows flee,
On the path of love, we find our key.

Each step a journey, each breath a prayer,
Guided by grace, beyond compare.
In the stillness, we hear His call,
On sacred ground, we rise, not fall.

With open hearts, we seek the divine,
In every moment, His love we find.
Through trials faced, our spirits grow,
In the dance of faith, His light we sow.

Serendipity and the Spirit

In the heart of chaos, peace is near,
Serendipity whispers, sweet and clear.
A gentle touch on weary souls,
In every twist, the spirit consoles.

Moments divine, grace intertwined,
The dance of fate, beautifully designed.
Every chance encounter, a sacred spark,
Illuminates the path through the dark.

With faith as our guide, we roam this earth,
Finding treasures in each little birth.
In the spirit's embrace, joy does ignite,
In serendipity, our hearts take flight.

Lessons Woven in Grace

In the fabric of life, lessons unfold,
Threads of compassion, stitch stories bold.
Each moment a canvas, painted with light,
In the tapestry of grace, shadows take flight.

Through trials we learn, through pain we grow,
In the heart's quiet whispers, love's warmth will flow.
The patterns of life, both harsh and sweet,
In lessons of grace, we find our feet.

With every heartbeat, wisdom flows deep,
In the sacred silence, our souls do leap.
In grace intertwined, we find our place,
Woven together, each lesson a trace.

The Covenant of Experience

In the book of life, each page we turn,
The covenant made, for wisdom we yearn.
Through joys and sorrows, our spirits align,
In experience shared, the sacred divine.

With open hands, we gather the days,
In laughter and tears, we walk in His ways.
Each moment a gift, each breath a song,
In the heart's embrace, we find where we belong.

The journey unfolds, a sacred decree,
In the dance of experience, we become free.
In unity's bond, we rise and we stand,
In the covenant of life, guided by His hand.

Lessons from the Stillness

In silence, wisdom softly speaks,
The heart finds peace in gentle creeks.
Where chaos fades, the spirit grows,
Awaiting truths that stillness knows.

In quiet moments, faith is sown,
A trust in paths we've yet to own.
With each breath, we draw nearer grace,
In stillness, we unveil His face.

Let go of fears, embrace the night,
For in the dark, we find the light.
The world may rush with frantic pace,
But in the calm, we find our place.

As nature whispers, souls unite,
In humble prayer, we seek the right.
From every pause, a lesson springs,
The quiet heart, a song that sings.

The Pilgrim's Path to Insight

With every step, a story told,
The pilgrim walks through trials bold.
Each stone a lesson, each hill a prayer,
In moments of doubt, we find His care.

The sky above, a guiding star,
Reminds us of how loved we are.
Through winding roads and tempest's call,
The heart learns softly, yet stands tall.

Beneath the weight of heavy load,
A strength is born upon this road.
For every tear, a blessing grows,
In every fear, His presence shows.

The path unfolds with every stride,
In faith, we learn to trust and bide.
With open hearts, we chase the light,
The pilgrim's way—a sacred rite.

Grace in the Shadows of Doubt

In shadows cast by whispered fears,
We seek the grace that wipes our tears.
Though doubts may linger, hearts will find,
In quiet grace, the light unlined.

A gentle touch in times of strife,
Reminds us of a deeper life.
For in the dark, His love does shine,
Transforming doubts to hope divine.

Each moment teeming with His care,
A beacon bright, forever there.
In struggles faced, a strength bestowed,
Through trials, true beliefs are sowed.

So rise, beloved, from shadows deep,
For grace will hold you while you sleep.
In every doubt, His presence dear,
In faith we walk, no need to fear.

Revelations Among the Stars

Beneath the stars, our spirits soar,
In constellations, we seek more.
Each twinkling light—a story shared,
Of ancient truths, divinely aired.

In night's embrace, the heart attunes,
To heavenly songs from distant moons.
Each glance above reveals His hand,
In whispers soft, we understand.

The universe, a sacred scroll,
Reveals the paths of every soul.
In cosmic dance, we find our fate,
A journey penned by love—so great.

From stardust dreams, we rise anew,
In galaxies, our faith rings true.
In revelations, hearts align,
Among the stars, His love divine.

The Art of Becoming Whole

In stillness we seek, a sacred breath,
Embracing the light that conquers death.
With open hearts, we mend the broken,
In each soft whisper, the truth is spoken.

Through trials faced, we rise anew,
Finding strength in what we pursue.
In divine grace, love's gentle hold,
A tapestry woven with threads of gold.

As shadows fade, the dawn draws near,
Each step we take, casting out fear.
Transforming pain into a song,
In unity's bond, we truly belong.

The journey unfolds, a path divine,
In every heartbeat, the stars align.
From darkness to light, we learn to flow,
In the art of becoming whole, we grow.

The spirit's journey, forever sought,
In moments of silence, wisdom is taught.
With open hands and hearts ablaze,
We walk in faith through life's endless maze.

The Bridge Between Questions

In the quiet hour, we ponder deep,
The mysteries of life, in shadows we seep.
With every question, a bridge is built,
Between the known and the unknown quilt.

In seeking truth, we find our place,
In every inquiry, there lies grace.
The heart shall guide where the mind may stray,
In the labyrinth of thought, we learn to pray.

What is the meaning of the path we tread?
A sacred dance where angels have led.
In the silence we listen, the answers flow,
In the heart of the seeker, the light will grow.

With each life chapter, a quest unfolds,
Stories of love and mysteries untold.
The bridge we cross, hand in hand,
In faith and hope, together we stand.

Through questions asked, we bloom and thrive,
In the space between, we come alive.
The journey continues, ever so bright,
For in every question, there shines a light.

Rituals of Reflection

In twilight's glow, we gather near,
To honor our journeys, each joy and tear.
With candlelight's warmth, we sit and share,
In every story, a glimpse of prayer.

We pause to reflect, in sacred time,
In whispers soft, our spirits climb.
With grateful hearts, we savor the past,
In the spirit's garden, our roots hold fast.

Through laughter and tears, a circle formed,
In vulnerability, we are transformed.
With every breath, we find release,
In rituals of reflection, we find peace.

As night deepens, the stars align,
Guiding our souls to the divine.
In unity's bond, our hearts ignite,
In the dance of love, we bask in the light.

From reflection's well, wisdom flows,
In the sacred space, our spirit grows.
With open minds, we seek to know,
In rituals of reflection, love will show.

A Symphony of Lessons

Life's melody plays, a timeless song,
In every note, where we belong.
Harmonies rise from discord and strife,
A symphony woven throughout our life.

In laughter and tears, we dance along,
Each moment a verse in the sacred throng.
With lessons learned, our spirits soar,
In love's embrace, we seek for more.

The cadence of time, ever so sweet,
In challenges faced, we find our beat.
With every trial, a tune unfolds,
In the symphony of lessons, our truth beholds.

As seasons change, the music flows,
In nature's rhythm, the wisdom glows.
Together we find strength in the sound,
In unity's chorus, our souls are found.

Through life's refrain, we sing our part,
In every whisper, the beat of the heart.
With gratitude sung, we rise above,
In this symphony of lessons, we learn of love.

The Alchemy of Surrender

In the stillness, hearts do yield,
Trusting grace, our wounds are healed.
With open hands, we let love flow,
An inner strength begins to grow.

Each tear released, a sacred song,
Guiding us where we belong.
In selfless acts, our spirits soar,
Finding peace on every shore.

In the shadows, we find the light,
A gentle whisper, guiding sight.
To surrender is to truly see,
The alchemy of what will be.

Through trials faced with faith so bright,
Every struggle ignites the night.
In trust we rise, like morning dew,
Transformed anew, in love so true.

Here we stand, in humble grace,
With open hearts to face our place.
In the dance of life, we learn to bend,
In this surrender, our souls ascend.

Beneath the Cloak of Mystery

Veiled in shadows, truth awaits,
Silent echoes, unlock the gates.
In the stillness, answers blend,
A divine force, our souls commend.

Follow whispers on the breeze,
Listen closely, hearts find ease.
In every path, the sacred weaves,
The cloak of mystery, love believes.

In each moment, wisdom dwells,
Beneath the surface, grace repels.
What we seek lies deep within,
A light that shines through every sin.

With each question a journey starts,
Connecting threads of myriad hearts.
In the unseen, we find our way,
Beneath the cloak of night and day.

Hold the mystery, cherish the quest,
In every trial, we are blessed.
In unity, with open minds,
The truth emerges, love entwined.

Illuminated Journeys of Faith

Through winding roads, our spirits roam,
Each step taken, leads us home.
With courage born from deep within,
Faith ignites the strength to begin.

Illuminated by a guiding star,
We walk through shadows, near and far.
With hearts ablaze, we embrace the night,
In every challenge, we find the light.

In moments small, and treasures deep,
Our dreams take flight, no time for sleep.
With every breath, a prayer we send,
In the journey, our hearts will mend.

As seasons change, our spirits grow,
With open hands, we reap what sow.
Each lesson learned, a sacred thread,
In faith's embrace, we're always led.

Let love be our guiding flame,
In the journey, none are the same.
Illuminate each step we take,
In faith's dance, our hearts awake.

The Silent Teacher Within

In quietude, the wisdom flows,
The silent teacher gently knows.
A sacred voice within our heart,
Unfolding truth, a work of art.

In still reflection, lessons rise,
Beneath the chatter, a soft surprise.
Each moment still, we come to see,
The sacred guide resides in me.

Listen closely, to the inner call,
In simple moments, we have it all.
With every breath, the pathway clears,
The silent teacher calms our fears.

Through trials faced, the soul expands,
In quietude, the heart understands.
With gentle grace, we learn to trust,
In stillness found, our spirits must.

So hold your heart with tender care,
For in the silence, love is rare.
The silent teacher whispers true,
In every moment, it speaks to you.

The Oracle of Experience

In silence whispers wisdom's call,
Through shadows dance where spirits fall.
Each step a tale, each breath a verse,
In trials deep, our truths immerse.

With open hearts, we seek the light,
The journey's path, both dark and bright.
In every sigh, in every tear,
The Oracle speaks, drawing near.

Through fire's test, we're forged anew,
In every scar, the strength we brew.
Past pain and joy, a sacred thread,
The tapestry of life is spread.

Awake, dear soul, to lessons learned,
In every page, the fire burned.
With arms spread wide, embrace the strife,
For in the struggle lies the life.

From heights of grace to valleys low,
The Oracle guides where we must go.
In echoes soft, our voices blend,
Experience whispers, wisdom's friend.

Harvesting Truth from Adversity

In parched fields where shadows loom,
From darkest nights, we find the bloom.
Resilience breeds in heavy rain,
From every storm, we rise again.

Truths buried deep in rugged soil,
Through hardship's grip, we cultivate toil.
Each struggle faced, a seed is sown,
In battles fought, our strength is grown.

With humble hearts, we glean the prize,
In sorrow's depths, the spirit flies.
The harvest rich, from pain we glean,
In every wound, the light is seen.

Giant shadows fade in the light,
As dawn breaks softly, conquering night.
From every tear, sweet wisdom flows,
In adversity, the spirit grows.

So stand firm through the tempests wild,
The path is hard, yet grace is mild.
With arms outstretched, the truth awaits,
In every trial, love resonates.

Treading the Waters of Understanding

In currents deep, the soul must wade,
With open hearts, our fears allayed.
Each wave a lesson, strong and clear,
In waters vast, we draw near.

The tide brings forth both joy and pain,
In every drop, a lesson gained.
Stepping stones through turbulent seas,
Understanding flows like gentle breeze.

With voices still, we seek to hear,
The whispers soft that draw us near.
In depths unknown, we seek the true,
The waters teach what we must do.

Challenge the waves, embrace the swell,
In storms of doubt, let courage dwell.
With every stroke, we navigate,
Through waters wide, we contemplate.

So tread with grace, and steadfast love,
In understanding, rise above.
For every challenge teaches us,
In soulful waters, we can trust.

The Sacred Palette of Life

With colors bright, the canvas sprawls,
Each stroke a story, life enthralls.
In diverse hues, our spirits dance,
The sacred palette gives us chance.

From whispers soft to thunder's roar,
Each moment crafted, memories soar.
In shades of hope, in tones of pain,
The artist's touch is never vain.

Brush in hand, we paint our fate,
With every choice, we create,
In fields of joy, in shadows grand,
The sacred art, a life well-planned.

So gather close all love and light,
Let laughter color darkest night.
In every stroke, seek unity,
For life's a canvas, ever free.

In the dance of color, find our way,
The sacred palette guides the day.
With every heartbeat, brush the strife,
In artful love, we find our life.

The Oasis of Pause

In the stillness, whispers rise,
A sanctuary where spirit lies.
Each heartbeat slows, a sacred song,
In this moment, we truly belong.

Beneath the sun, the shadows play,
Mountains of worry gently sway.
With every breath, the soul refreshes,
In the warm embrace, the heart confesses.

Time drifts softly, a gentle stream,
In the oasis, we dare to dream.
The sands of doubt begin to fade,
In this quiet, faith is made.

Minds unburdened, spirits free,
In this pause, we simply be.
Among the palms, our troubles cease,
Finding in stillness, a path to peace.

Let us gather, hand in hand,
In this sacred, holy land.
With hearts that beckon and souls that share,
The oasis waits, our breath of prayer.

The Mirror of the Infinite

In the depths where silence dwells,
A reflection of truth gently swells.
Every thought, a ripple cast,
In the mirror, the future and past.

Through the glass, the cosmos sings,
Revelations born on shimmering wings.
Every star, a whisper bright,
Guiding the heart from darkness to light.

As we gaze into the expanse,
We see the echoes of life's dance.
Heartbeats collide, time intertwines,
In the infinite, the divine aligns.

Let the mirror show your grace,
Illuminate the sacred space.
In every glance, the soul confides,
Reflecting love that never hides.

As we wander, hand in hand,
In the infinite, we understand.
Every moment, a sacred rhyme,
In the mirror, we transcend time.

Beneath the Surface of Silence

In the hush where the heart reflects,
Whispers of wisdom the spirit expects.
Beneath still waters, secrets flow,
With every silence, the truth will grow.

Soft shadows cradle our deepest fears,
In the quiet, echoing prayers.
Listen closely; the soul's embrace,
In the stillness, we find our place.

Time pauses here, in sacred space,
Each heartbeat echoes grace's face.
Beneath the surface, ripples part,
In silence, we hear the voice of the heart.

Within this calm, our spirits soar,
Finding peace on the timeless shore.
The depths hold stories, waiting to rise,
Revealing the beauty within the guise.

Come, let us dive into the quiet,
In the silence, our souls ignite.
Beneath the surface, we are one,
In this stillness, our journey begun.

The Journey of the Seeker

In the quest where shadows blend,
The seeker wanders, heart to mend.
With every step, the light unfolds,
In the journey, the truth beholds.

Across the mountains, through the trees,
The whispers of wisdom ride the breeze.
Each path reveals a lesson shared,
In every challenge, the spirit's bared.

The stars above, a guiding light,
Illuminating the path of the night.
In the labyrinth of dreams and fate,
The seeker finds the open gate.

With open heart and curious mind,
In every moment, the divine aligned.
Through valleys low and peaks that gleam,
The journey weaves a sacred dream.

So take this path, embrace the call,
In the seeker's quest, we weave it all.
In each step, the purpose clear,
The journey of the seeker draws us near.

Divine Whispers of Understanding

In the silence, hear the call,
A gentle breeze that stirs the soul.
Wisdom flows like a sacred stream,
In every heart, a hidden dream.

Stars above twinkle like eyes,
Watching over as time flies.
Each moment, a gift divine,
In every breath, His love will shine.

As faith takes root in fertile ground,
In shadows deep, His grace is found.
Through trials and tears, love will grow,
In hardship's face, His presence glows.

Listen closely, the truths unfold,
In whispered tales of the ages old.
With open heart, let spirit soar,
In the light of love, forevermore.

So walk in reverence, hand in hand,
With the Divine, take your stand.
Each step a prayer, each word a song,
In unity, we all belong.

The Light Through the Veil

Beyond the shadows, a soft glow,
A beacon bright, where spirits flow.
Veils of sorrow, lifted high,
To reveal the truth that will not die.

In quiet moments, hearts ignite,
Guided gently by the light.
Hope and faith, like morning dew,
Awake the soul to something new.

Every tear, a lesson learned,
In the furnace, the spirit burned.
Through pain, we find our way,
The light will break, the night will sway.

Feel the warmth of love's embrace,
Let it fill your sacred space.
In the stillness, whispers sing,
Of the joy that surrender brings.

So journey forth, with heart ablaze,
In every moment, lift your praise.
The veil grows thin; the truth revealed,
In the light of love, we are healed.

In the Garden of Reflection

Amidst the blooms, in quiet earth,
Discovering the sacred worth.
Petals whisper tales of grace,
In every corner, His warm embrace.

The breeze carries prayers on high,
A symphony within the sky.
Seeds of faith in soil are sown,
In this garden, we feel at home.

Mirror of truth, the waters gleam,
Reflecting all our hopes and dreams.
In the stillness, we cultivate,
A bond with love that won't abate.

As moonlight dances on the leaves,
In each heartbeat, the spirit weaves.
Through the shadows, we seek the sun,
In harmony, we are one.

So dwell here, in this sacred space,
With open hearts, and boundless grace.
In the garden, blossoms thrive,
With faith and love, our souls alive.

Sacred Echoes of the Soul

In the chambers of the heart, we find,
Sacred echoes, intertwined.
Whispers soft, they call our name,
In every pulse, a sacred flame.

Journey deep, where silence reigns,
Understand the joy, the pains.
Each heartbeat a song divine,
In unity, our spirits shine.

Mountains high and valleys low,
In every step, the truth will flow.
Lessons learned from past to now,
In reverence, we take a vow.

Through the ages, love remains,
Breaking every chain that strains.
In the tapestry of the night,
Stars will guide us with their light.

Embrace the echoes, let them lead,
In every heart, their whispers seed.
With faith as our eternal goal,
We dance together, soul to soul.

The Divine Script of Understanding

In the stillness of the night,
Whispers of truth take flight.
Hearts open wide to grace,
In every shadow, find His face.

Guided by the sacred light,
We walk together, in His sight.
Each step a humble prayer,
Through trials, Love is always there.

Teach us to see with open eyes,
To hear the truth beyond the lies.
In every word, a holy sound,
In silence, deeper peace is found.

The journey leads to wise hearts,
Where kindness blooms and never departs.
Embrace the path, where faith aligns,
In this Divine script, love defines.

Let compassion guide our ways,
In every moment, let us praise.
Together we rise, hand in hand,
In unity, forever we stand.

The Blooming of the Spirit

In the garden of the soul,
Seeds of hope begin to roll.
Nurtured by the gentle rain,
Love's soft whispers soothe our pain.

Petals unfold to greet the dawn,
In each heartbeat, strength is drawn.
With faith as roots, we reach for light,
In darkness, we find our sight.

Let joy arise, a fragrant breeze,
In stillness, find our inner peace.
As the spirit starts to bloom,
The heart expands, dispelling gloom.

With every prayer, we sway and dance,
Entrusted to this holy chance.
The tapestry of life we weave,
In gratitude, we truly believe.

Together, let us rise and sing,
Of all the love that faith will bring.
In harmony, our spirits soar,
With open hearts, we seek and explore.

In Search of the Sacred Wisdom

Through mountains high and valleys low,
In every breath, the Spirit flows.
Wisdom whispers in the breeze,
In quietude, the heart finds ease.

With each question, the soul ignites,
Illuminating the darkest nights.
A compass forged from holy dreams,
In silence, we hear the sacred themes.

Stories of old guide our way,
In every challenge, let us pray.
For wisdom seeks the humble heart,
In love's embrace, we play our part.

Each page turned, a lesson learned,
As candles flicker, brightly burned.
Seeking truth in each endeavor,
In spirit, we stay united forever.

The journey's path is never straight,
In surrender, we find our fate.
With open hearts, we seek to find,
The sacred wisdom, intertwined.

The Parables Hidden in Everyday Life

In simple acts, the wisdom lies,
A gentle touch, a soft surprise.
In laughter shared, in tears we find,
A glimpse of Love, both kind and blind.

Nature speaks in whispered tones,
In rustling leaves, the heart atones.
Each moment holds a parable true,
In service, love shines bright and new.

Through trials faced with heads held high,
Resilience born from deep inside.
Each story shared around the fire,
We weave the truth, our hearts inspire.

The everyday reveals what's grand,
In simple grace, we understand.
In every smile, a light will spark,
Love's luminous flame igniting the dark.

So let us walk with open eyes,
To see the holy in the skies.
In every moment, hear the call,
In life's parables, we find it all.

The Light at the End of the Labyrinth

In shadows deep where lost souls roam,
The flickering flame calls us home.
With whispers soft and guiding light,
It leads us from the endless night.

Through winding paths of doubt and fear,
The heart's true compass draws us near.
Each step a prayer, a chance to rise,
To find our truth beyond the lies.

In the maze of life, we seek to find,
The gentle hand that soothes the mind.
With courage born of love's embrace,
We walk unchained in sacred grace.

The light awaits at every turn,
Its warmth ignites a holy burn.
A beacon bright, our spirits soar,
Through trials faced, we learn to roar.

So take my hand, dear wanderer true,
Together we'll find what's given due.
The light will guide, as hope ascends,
Through labyrinths, our journey bends.

The Watchful Eye of Existence

In silence deep, the heavens gaze,
Upon our lives, through night's dark haze.
Each moment held with careful grace,
The watchful eye, our sacred space.

With every breath, a prayer takes flight,
A spark ignites in darkest night.
In joy and pain, in growth and loss,
The eye observes, no burdens cross.

Wisdom flows from unseen hands,
Through time and tide, we make our stands.
In laughter loud or tearful sighs,
The watchful eye, where love complies.

As seasons change and shadows fade,
In every choice, a path we've laid.
Eternal gaze with patience rare,
Embraces all, through joy and care.

Lift up your gaze, and you shall see,
The woven thread of destiny.
In unity, through all that's deemed,\nWe find the truth in what we've dreamed.

In Praise of Life's Lessons

Oh, sacred life, with trials profound,
In every lesson, wisdom's found.
Each step we take, each choice we make,
A verse of love, no heart can break.

Through stormy skies and tranquil days,
We learn to walk in myriad ways.
Each stumble teaches, each fall uplifts,
In moments lost, the soul still sifts.

Gratitude blooms in gardens rare,
For struggles met with gentle care.
In joy we dance, in sorrow we sing,
Life's lessons shape the heart, they bring.

Embrace the journey, the twists and bends,
For every chapter, the spirit mends.
In praise we rise, as phoenix reborn,
From ashes scattered, new paths are worn.

So heed the call, let love unfurl,
In life's grand tapestry, find your pearl.
With open hearts and minds embraced,
In every lesson, a truth is traced.

The Mosaic of Understanding

In fragmented pieces, we find our way,
Colors of life in bright array.
Each shard a story, each hue a truth,
Crafting a vision from the roots of youth.

From varied paths, diverse in thought,
The wisdom gained cannot be bought.
In dialogues rich, with patience and grace,
The mosaic forms in a sacred space.

Unity blooms where differences meet,
In dialogues shared, our hearts repeat.
With open minds and spirits free,
Understanding blooms, as vast as the sea.

A tapestry woven with threads of care,
In each connection, we learn to share.
Our world enriched by every stitch,
In harmony's song, we find our niche.

So gather 'round, let stories unfold,
With every voice, a truth retold.
The mosaic shines with colors bright,
In unity's embrace, we share the light.

Parables of the Soul

In silence, the soul seeks light,
Whispers of truth guide the night.
Each heart a vessel, longing to know,
The path of love where gentle winds blow.

In shadows cast by doubt and fear,
Faith blooms softly, drawing us near.
Through trials faced, we learn to rise,
In every sorrow, a blessing lies.

The still small voice within us speaks,
In every moment, grace it seeks.
With every tear, a lesson learned,
For every flame, a heart that burned.

In the garden where hope is sown,
Compassion's seeds find fertile stone.
Together we walk, hand in hand,
United in spirit, across the land.

As stars illuminate the dark,
Each soul a flame, a sacred spark.
In unity, we find our role,
A symphony written for the soul.

The Gospel of Existence

Life's sacred pages, filled with grace,
Every moment a warm embrace.
In trials faced, we find our truth,
Each heartbeat echoes wisdom's youth.

Through valleys deep and mountains high,
With faith as wings, we learn to fly.
In unity, we stand as one,
Beneath the light of the rising sun.

The gospel of love, a timeless tale,
Guides our hearts when we feel frail.
In every gesture, a chance to heal,
A promise of hope, forever real.

In connection, we find our peace,
Through shared stories, our sorrows cease.
Understanding blooms like flowers bright,
In the garden of spirit, pure delight.

In every breath, eternity sings,
Embracing the joy that each moment brings.
Through laughter and tears, we weave our lore,
In the gospel of existence, forevermore.

Prayers Penned in Life's Notebook

In every line, a lover's plea,
Written softly for the world to see.
With ink of hope on pages bare,
Faithful whispers dance in the air.

Each word a step on sacred ground,
In life's great journey, love is found.
With gratitude, we pen our days,
In the warmth of truth, our hearts ablaze.

As prayers rise like morning dew,
In humble voices, we seek what's true.
Finding strength in quiet grace,
In life's vast story, we embrace.

With open hearts, we share our dreams,
Guided by light, or so it seems.
In every struggle, there's a prayer,
Within the battles, love's repair.

As pages turn, the journey flows,
In life's notebook, our spirit glows.
In every prayer, a bond we share,
Through life's passage, love is there.

Celestial Echoes of Experience

Stars whisper secrets in the night,
Echoes of wisdom, pure and bright.
Through trials faced in earthly realms,
We gather strength as love overwhelms.

In every heartbeat, stories weave,
Of hopes and dreams, we dare believe.
Celestial notes fill the vast expanse,
As the universe invites us to dance.

In sacred spaces, souls collide,
In shared moments, we must abide.
Each echo a reminder to be,
An integral part of eternity.

Beneath the heavens, we chart our course,
With faith as our ever-guiding force.
In the tapestry of time, we find,
A melody shared, a bond that's blind.

With gratitude, we heed the call,
In celestial echoes, we rise where we fall.
For every experience, a lesson learned,
In the heart's embrace, our spirit burned.

The Lessons Woven by Faith

In quiet whispers, hope resides,
Through trials faced, the spirit guides.
Each tear a lesson, each sorrow a prayer,
Faith's gentle hand leads us there.

With every step, the path unfolds,
In sacred stories, the truth retolds.
Beneath the burden, we find the grace,
In love's embrace, we find our place.

The sun will rise after the storm,
In darkest nights, our hearts stay warm.
Woven in love, our spirits sing,
In unity, together we bring.

With every doubt, a seed is sown,
In trust we bloom, no longer alone.
Strength found in the hands of the weak,
Through grace divine, we dare to speak.

Through avenues of faith we walk,
In every silence, our hearts will talk.
Lessons woven, eternally bright,
Guided always by inner light.

From Shadows to Sacred Light

In shadows cast by fear and doubt,
Faith's soft glow will call us out.
Through winding paths where loss has tread,
The light of love is gently spread.

In morning's light, the heart will dare,
To seek the rise of hope laid bare.
What once was lost, now shines anew,
As grace unfolds in every view.

When burdens weigh and spirits fall,
In sacred moments, we hear the call.
Transcending pain, we break the night,
Emerging strong into the light.

With every tear, a spark ignites,
A journey forged in sacred rites.
From shadows deep, our souls take flight,
Embraced by love, we find our sight.

In life's tapestry, we weave and flow,
Connecting hearts in love's warm glow.
From shadows deep, we rise and fight,
Arrayed in love, our spirits bright.

Beneath the Crossroads of Belief

At the crossroads, we stand aligned,
In faith we gather, hearts entwined.
With choices laid, we seek the way,
Guided by love, come what may.

In every doubt, there lies a flame,
A spark of hope, a sacred name.
With open hearts, we face the night,
Gathering strength in the holy light.

Each path diverges, but leads to grace,
In gentle hands, our fears we place.
We journey forth, with hearts so bold,
In stories shared, our truth unfolds.

Through trials borne, we find the peace,
In every wound, a chance for release.
With every step, we learn to see,
The beauty woven in unity.

Beneath the sky, the spirit soars,
In every heartbeat, love implores.
At the crossroads, we stand as one,
Embracing life 'til the race is run.

The Testament of Trials

In trials deep, our faith is forged,
Through tempest fierce, our spirits surged.
Each challenge faced, a story penned,
The testament of love transcends.

With heavy hearts, we lean on grace,
Transforming pain, we find our place.
In every scar, a tale reveals,
The strength of love, it never steals.

Through fire we walk, and yet we rise,
In every tear, a new sunrise.
Our journey shared, through thick and thin,
In faith's embrace, we find our kin.

With steadfast hearts, we bear the load,
In trials faced, we find our road.
Each step we take brings wisdom bright,
Guided by faith, we chase the light.

In woven tales, our lives combined,
In every lesson, the love we find.
The testament of trials won,
In every heart, we are but one.

The Alchemy of Experience

In the journey of soul and heart,
Lessons born from pain and grace,
Each moment a sacred art,
Transforming shadows to a brighter place.

With every stumble, wisdom grows,
Gilded thoughts from trials faced,
The path reveals what stillness shows,
In the crucible of life embraced.

Time weaves the threads of days gone by,
In faith, we find the strength to stand,
An inner fire that will not die,
Crafting joy with a careful hand.

Each tear a gem, each laugh a praise,
In suffering, beauty can be found,
Illuminate the darkest maze,
Where love and light together abound.

So trust the journey's winding road,
For in the struggle, grace is born,
The alchemy of life's deep code,
Turns sorrow's night to dawning morn.

Revelations in the Quiet Moments

In silence, whispers softly sway,
The heart's truth dances in the still,
In moments carved from light of day,
Revealing paths the spirit will.

Open ears to the sacred call,
Where nature breathes a breath of peace,
Within the quiet, we grow tall,
And find in stillness, sweet release.

Each breath a prayer, each thought a song,
In the calm, the soul begins to see,
A tapestry where all belong,
And love unites the you and me.

The dawn unfolds in gentle hues,
As shadows fade with morning light,
Each fleeting moment offers clues,
To guide our steps from night to bright.

So cherish each serene embrace,
For in the calm, the truth ignites,
Revelations in the quiet space,
Where spirit soars into the heights.

When the Spirit Speaks

In stillness found beyond the noise,
The spirit whispers, soft and clear,
A knowing that restores our joys,
In every laugh, in every tear.

It calls us to the path of light,
Where love cascades like rivers flow,
Through darkest valleys, shining bright,
A guiding voice that we all know.

When burdens weigh upon the heart,
Listen close, let silence reign,
In our surrender, we take part,
In wisdom born from joy and pain.

So heed the echoes in the deep,
Embrace the lessons gently shared,
For when the spirit stirs from sleep,
We find the dreams for which we've dared.

Let every prayer arise in faith,
For in this dance, divinity,
Awakens us, reveals our grace,
And breathes in us, eternally.

The Sacred Tapestry of Truth

Threads of life, a tapestry spun,
Woven by hands both strong and frail,
In every color, sorrows run,
Yet joy, like light, will always prevail.

Each strand a story, each hue a prayer,
In the fabric of existence divined,
Interwoven fates, the burdens we bear,
Together, our souls are soulfully lined.

From hardships faced, we learn to soar,
In woven tales of love's embrace,
Every tear a stitch, every roar,
Crafts beauty through the darkest place.

So let us cherish every thread,
In unity, the truth displayed,
For in this sacred weave, we're led,
To understand the part we played.

In the tapestry of time and fate,
The sacred echoes never cease,
With every moment, we create,
A masterpiece of love and peace.

An Offering of Insight

In the quiet of the dawn, we seek,
A whisper from the heavens, so unique.
With open hearts and hands held high,
We gather strength, let our spirits fly.

In the stillness, wisdom flows,
Guiding paths where love bestows.
With every prayer, a seed is sown,
In faith's embrace, we are not alone.

In the tapestry of life, we weave,
Threads of hope, we believe.
As shadows dance, the light will break,
In this truth, our souls awake.

Through trials faced and burdens shared,
A bond is formed, a love declared.
With gratitude, we lift our voice,
In the silence, we rejoice.

Embrace the power, the gift of grace,
In every heart, find your place.
Together we rise, together we stand,
In unity, a sacred band.

From Ashes to Enlightenment

From the ashes, hope takes flight,
Restoring faith, igniting the night.
In every struggle, lessons learned,
Through trials faced, our spirits burned.

In the depth of sorrow, a spark ignites,
Transcending pain, we reach new heights.
The embers glow with truths divine,
From darkness, we emerge, we shine.

Whispers of courage guide the way,
Leading us from night to day.
In the garden of our soul's desire,
We rise anew, we lift each other higher.

With every step, we walk in light,
Bound by love, prepared to fight.
From ashes, beauty springs anew,
In gratitude, we find our view.

As phoenix flies, so shall we soar,
In unity, we find the core.
Through every storm, we find release,
From ashes born, our hearts in peace.

The Scrolls of the Heart

In the depths of the heart, a story lies,
Whispered softly, beneath the skies.
With every beat, a truth unfolds,
The scrolls of life, precious and bold.

Each page a moment, each line a breath,
In love's embrace, we conquer death.
With ink of faith, we write our tale,
In the winds of time, we shall prevail.

Through joy and sorrow, we journey on,
In every dawn, a new song.
With hands entwined, we share our fears,
In silence, we gather the tears.

In celebration, we lift our praise,
For every moment, we cherish our days.
With gratitude, our spirits rise,
In the scrolls of the heart, love never dies.

We write our legacy with grace and care,
In every heartbeat, a sacred prayer.
With each chapter, a lesson learned,
In the scrolls of the heart, our passion burned.

Wisdom Born of Struggle

In the furnace of life, we are refined,
Through trials faced, our souls aligned.
In darkness, we find the light,
With every battle, we gain our sight.

From every wound, strength does arise,
A testament to the tenacious ties.
With every scar, a story shared,
In the heart's resilience, we've prepared.

In the whisper of pain, there is grace,
Guiding us through the toughest place.
With open arms, we embrace the fight,
In the struggle's shadows, we find the light.

Through clouds of doubt, we find our way,
Each step forward, a brighter day.
In unity, we share the load,
In every heart, love's abode.

With wisdom gained, we rise anew,
Through struggle faced, our spirits grew.
In every heartbeat, we find the proof,
Of love enduring, steadfast truth.

Threads of a Divine Narrative

In the tapestry of light, we weave,
Each thread a prayer, a heart that believes.
With faith as our needle, we stitch the grace,
In the loom of existence, we find our place.

Through trials and triumphs, we learn to trust,
In sacred moments, divine paths adjust.
The stories unfold, like petals in bloom,
Illuminating truths that dispel the gloom.

Every tear that falls, a seed sown deep,
In the soil of our souls, where mysteries keep.
With the whispers of angels, we hear the call,
In the threads of our lives, we rise and fall.

The dance of creation, a celestial hymn,
Guiding our spirits, when light seems dim.
Through the shadows, a promise shines bright,
A reminder of love, an eternal light.

So in unity, let us weave and mend,
Threads of compassion, on which we depend.
In our hearts, may the narrative grow,
A divine tapestry, forever aglow.

The Womb of Wisdom

In the silence of night, wisdom resides,
A nurturing force, where the spirit guides.
Here in the stillness, the heart finds its breath,
Cradled in love, away from all death.

The womb of creation, a sacred embrace,
Where the seeds of knowledge find their place.
In the warmth of the spirit, we learn and unfold,
The truths that sustain, the stories retold.

Every question asked, a journey begun,
In the realm of the heart, we are all one.
With patience and grace, we open our sight,
Finding the answers that dance in the light.

Through valleys of doubt, we wander so far,
Yet wisdom will guide us, a luminous star.
In the depths of our being, we seek and we find,
The womb of wisdom, forever entwined.

So let us be mindful of the lessons that flow,
In the garden of heart, where true insights grow.
Embracing the stillness, our fears will subside,
In the womb of wisdom, we ever abide.

Serene Ponderings

In the quiet of dawn, thoughts gently arise,
Whispers of grace dance before our eyes.
Holding the moment, we breathe in the peace,
A canvas of stillness, where conflicts cease.

In reflection we ponder, the mysteries vast,
Learning from shadows, forgiving the past.
Each heartbeat a lesson, a rhythm divine,
In the silence we gather, true love we define.

Through valleys of thought, our spirits will roam,
Finding the solace that calls us back home.
In the lapping of waves and the rustle of leaves,
Serene ponderings cradle everything we believe.

With open hearts, we explore the unknown,
Seeking the essence of seeds that we've sown.
Though storms may arise, the soul finds its way,
In the tranquil embrace of each dawning day.

So let us be gentle, and listen within,
To the whispers of peace that invite us to win.
In the garden of thought, let compassion bloom,
In serene ponderings, alive to each tune.

The Garden of Celestial Lessons

Beneath the wide sky, a garden so fair,
Each flower a lesson, each breeze a prayer.
In this sacred space, we wander and grow,
Harvesting wisdom from seeds we forego.

The sun shines upon us, illuminating all,
From the tiniest bloom to the grandest tall.
In the laughter of streams, in the hush of the trees,
We find the connections, the gentle heart's ease.

In shadows we dwell, as the day turns to dusk,
Yet the night brings its stars, in wonder we trust.
With each star that twinkles, a story unfolds,
The garden's deep secrets begin to be told.

With patience we nurture, our spirits take flight,
In the garden of lessons, we find our true light.
Together we cultivate, hand in hand,
The beauty of growth in this vast, loving land.

So let us rejoice in the blooms that appear,
In the garden of celestial lessons so dear.
For every experience, a gift from above,
A tapestry woven with faith and with love.

Through the Lens of Grace

In shadows deep, where lost souls roam,
A gentle light calls them back home.
With every tear and whispered prayer,
Grace flows freely, lifting despair.

In humble hearts, the truth unfolds,
The gift of mercy, a story retold.
Though worn by trials, with scars we bear,
We find redemption in love's sweet care.

Each moment glimmers, a sacred chance,
To weave our pain into His dance.
The veil of doubt begins to fade,
In faith's embrace, our fears are laid.

Through every struggle, through every fall,
His hands will catch us, we hear the call.
In the chaos of life, we find our place,
As we see the world through the lens of grace.

So let your spirit rise like the morn,
In the light of love, we're reborn.
With every heartbeat, trust and believe,
In the power of grace, we shall receive.

The Serpent and the Flame

In Eden's garden where shadows creep,
The serpent whispered secrets deep.
With every bite, innocence fell,
And sin's cold grasp forged our hell.

Yet from the ashes, a fire was born,
A flame that shone through darkest morn.
In trials fierce, we rise, we claim,
The gift of hope within His name.

From thorns and briars, a crown does bloom,
Worn by the One who bore our doom.
His blood, our solace, in pain and strife,
Transforms our death into eternal life.

In bitter battles, let courage rise,
For even serpents can't disguise.
With hearts ablaze, we shall proclaim,
Our love for Him, a holy flame.

So turn from shadow, embrace the light,
In faith's embrace, we find our sight.
With every breath, let praise take aim,
In the war of souls, ignite the flame.

Seeking the Divine in the Mundane

In daily toil and simple hours,
We seek the sacred in blooming flowers.
In cups of tea and laughter shared,
The divine whispers, reminding we cared.

In chores and tasks, His presence glows,
In every gesture, His love bestows.
With weary hands and tender grace,
We find His spirit in every place.

In morning sun and evening skies,
His beauty shines in earthly ties.
Amidst the noise, His voice we hear,
In silent moments, we draw near.

In hearts surrendered, the mundane shifts,
Into sacred ground where the spirit lifts.
Through every breath, we come alive,
In the simple things, the divine thrives.

So let us walk with open eyes,
And find His love in each sunrise.
In ordinary life, let us proclaim,
The beauty of seeking in His name.

Illuminated Footprints on Earth

Upon the path where shadows play,
Illuminated footprints guide our way.
Each step we take echoes His call,
With gentle love, we shall not fall.

In whispered winds, the sacred speaks,
In valleys low and mountain peaks.
With every heartbeat, His grace we trace,
In the tapestry of time and space.

Through trials fierce, He walks beside,
Our doubts and fears, He'll gently guide.
In faith's embrace, we rise anew,
With every challenge, His strength shines through.

So let us follow with hearts on fire,
In service, love, and endless desire.
From earth to heaven, our spirits soar,
In illuminated footprints, we seek more.

Together we journey, hand in hand,
As bearers of light across the land.
With every step, let us proclaim,
His love and light in His holy name.

The Singularity of Faith's Path

In the quiet night, faith ignites,
Guiding hearts through endless sights.
Each step forward, a sacred light,
With every doubt, a silent fight.

Beneath the stars, the spirit soars,
Embracing truths behind closed doors.
In the depths, the soul explores,
Unwavering love, the heart restores.

Paths entwined in grace divine,
Trust in the way that feels like home.
In every whisper, soft and fine,
We find our place, no need to roam.

The journey calls, each soul unique,
In the sharing, we find our peak.
Through trials faced, the strong not weak,
United in the love we seek.

And when the dawn unveils the day,
We walk with faith, come what may.
Each moment cherished, come what stays,
In the singular path, we find our way.

Chronicles of Transformation

In shadows deep, the fire ignites,
From ashes rise, new hopes take flight.
Beneath the pain, a strength ignites,
In the soil of tears, blooms the light.

The heart, a canvas, truth displayed,
Every mark, a promise made.
Through stormy nights, we are remade,
In brokenness, His love conveyed.

Echoes of grace in each soft breath,
Lessons learned through life and death.
In every heartbeat, we are blessed,
Transformed by faith, the soul's deep quest.

Each moment holds a sacred vow,
In trusting Him, we stand somehow.
With every trial, we humbly bow,
In transformation, we know Him now.

As dawn breaks forth, we rise anew,
Guided by light, our spirits true.
From darkness' clutch, we find our view,
In chronicles bright, love will ensue.

The Teaching Trees of Life

In the forest deep, wisdom grows,
With branches wide, and roots that know.
Each rustling leaf, a story shows,
Of life's embrace, as time bestows.

The trees stand tall, in silence speak,
Of seasons endured, of strength they seek.
In every ring, a lesson deep,
In shadows cast, and promises keep.

Through storms they bend, yet never break,
A testament to all that's at stake.
In the stillness, their whispers wake,
Reminding souls, of love's embrace.

Gather beneath the leafy dome,
In sacred space, we find our home.
With every breath, our spirits roam,
In teaching trees, our hearts become.

As nature sings, a choir sublime,
In harmony with the pulse of time.
Rooted in love, we find the rhyme,
In the teaching trees, our lives align.

The Soul's Whisper in Stillness

In quiet moments, whispers dwell,
Softly calling, breaking the shell.
Within the calm, the spirit swells,
In every heartbeat, truth compels.

The stillness speaks, with gentle grace,
Finding peace in a sacred space.
In solitude, we seek His face,
With every breath, a warm embrace.

In the depths, where silence lies,
The soul's true voice forever flies.
A sacred song in moonlit skies,
In stillness found, our spirit sighs.

With simple joys and humble praise,
We greet the dawn in golden rays.
In every moment, love displays,
In the soul's whisper, the heart obeys.

As time unfolds, we learn to see,
In stillness great, we are set free.
With quiet faith, we cease to flee,
In the soul's whisper, we simply be.

Wisdom Carved by Silent Prayer

In the hush of dawn's first light,
Whispers rise, hearts take flight.
Hands clasped tight, seeking grace,
In silence, we find our place.

The soul's soft sigh, a sacred sound,
In stillness, true wisdom is found.
Every tear a pearl of truth,
Each prayer a bridge to eternal youth.

Guided by faith, we tread the path,
In humble hearts, love ignites the wrath.
Casting doubts like shadows away,
When we trust, we boldly sway.

In the quiet, strength will grow,
Forging insight in the glow.
With each breath, we draw near,
Carved by prayer, banishing fear.

The echoes linger, softly speak,
In sacred stillness, we grow meek.
Bearing the light, we share the flame,
Wisdom carved, in His holy name.

Beneath the Veil of Understanding

Veiled by doubts, we strain to see,
Yet the heart whispers, we must be free.
Layers of life, masked in disguise,
Truth unfolds, as the spirit flies.

Beneath the veil, the light unfurls,
In moments still, compassion swirls.
Every question a path to grace,
In unity, we find our space.

With open eyes, we glimpse the wise,
Understanding dawns, as love applies.
Each soul a mirror, reflecting light,
Together we rise, igniting the night.

The journey inward, often unseen,
Brings forth the spirit, pure and serene.
What binds us all is kindness shared,
In tenderness, we are prepared.

To lift the veil and simply feel,
Every heartbeat, a sacred deal.
Beneath the surface, truth does dwell,
In understanding, all is well.

The Holy Journey Within

With every step, the path unfolds,
A journey sacred, a story told.
Within our hearts, the light ignites,
A pilgrimage of gentle sights.

The valleys low, the mountains high,
In struggle's grip, we learn to fly.
With faith as our compass, we press on,
Toward horizons bright, till fears are gone.

In quiet moments, the spirit speaks,
Guiding through the trials and peaks.
Each revelation, a gentle gift,
In the holy journey, our souls uplift.

Sacred whispers echo deep,
In the silence, promises we keep.
The flame of hope forever glows,
As the heart, to the heavens, flows.

This odyssey, a dance divine,
Finding treasure in every sign.
In gratitude, we walk the way,
The holy journey blooms each day.

Illuminated by Trials

Through shadows deep, the spirit grows,
In the crucible, true strength shows.
Every trial, a lesson learned,
In the fires, the heart is turned.

Bathed in struggle, souls arise,
Chasing storms, embracing skies.
With every challenge that we face,
We carve our path, we find our place.

In tears of sorrow, bridges built,
The wounds of life, a canvas spilt.
From ashes, hope does rise anew,
Illuminated, the spirit true.

Together, we gather in the fight,
Each scar a testament of light.
With faith intact, we rise and sing,
The trials, a blessing they bring.

In unity's embrace, we shine,
Transcending limits, hearts entwined.
With every step, we break the chains,
Illuminated by sacred gains.

Under the Eye of Providence

In shadows cast by sacred light,
We walk our paths, well-drained of fright.
With faith as our unwavering guide,
We stand together, side by side.

For every tear, a lesson sown,
In trials, our true selves are shown.
The Eye of Grace watches with care,
In moments dark, we find Him there.

In every heartbeat, whispers blessed,
A call to rise, to seek, to rest.
Through storms that rage and winds that pry,
We hold the truth, we will not die.

The stars proclaim His wondrous might,
In silent prayers during the night.
With every dawn, new hope appears,
In His embrace, we shed our fears.

So let us walk with heads held high,
Beneath the vast and sacred sky.
In unity, our spirits soar,
Under the Eye forevermore.

Lessons Written in the Sand

Upon the shore where tides do meet,
God writes His words, both true and sweet.
As waves will crash and pull away,
So do our doubts and fears decay.

In grains of sand, our stories lie,
Each moment fleeting, like the sky.
With every stride, we shape our fate,
His love endures, it will not wait.

When storms arise and shadows loom,
We find His light within the gloom.
Each lesson carved in time's embrace,
A testament to boundless grace.

In whispers soft, He calls our name,
With gentle touch, He fuels the flame.
From ashes rise, like phoenix flight,
His hand will guide us through the night.

So let us tread upon this shore,
And seek each truth He has in store.
For every step upon the sand,
Is written by His mighty hand.

The Flow of Benevolent Currents

The river flows with purpose grand,
A stream of love from His own hand.
Through valleys deep and mountains high,
His grace cascades, a gentle sigh.

In currents strong, we find our way,
Through trials faced and dreams at bay.
Though rocks may form our paths unknown,
We navigate by faith alone.

For in the depths of every strife,
We drink the nectar of His life.
His wisdom flows like crystal streams,
Refreshes souls, ignites our dreams.

The waters whisper truths profound,
In every ripple, grace abounds.
Through trials faced beneath the sky,
His current leads, we rise on high.

So let us sail with hearts aflame,
Embrace the flow, exalt His name.
For in His streams, we find our peace,
In every drop, His love will cease.

Wisdom's Embrace in the Storm

In tempest's heart, where shadows cling,
Wisdom speaks, and angels sing.
Through raging skies and thunder's roar,
His gentle call is evermore.

In chaos found, His voice we hear,
A guiding light to calm our fear.
With every gust, His hand extends,
In storms of life, true love transcends.

Though waves may crash and darkness chase,
We stand protected in His grace.
Each raindrop falls, a lesson learned,
For in the fire, our hearts are burned.

So take my hand when winds arise,
Together, we shall seize the skies.
For in the storm, a truth remains,
His wisdom soothes, our hope sustains.

Through tempests fierce, with faith we hold,
In Wisdom's arms, our hearts unfold.
For even in the fiercest night,
His love will guide us to the light.

The Language of the Heart's Journey

In whispers soft as morning dew,
Hearts convey the path we tread.
Each step an echo of the true,
In faith, we forge where souls are led.

Through valleys deep and mountains high,
The spirit sings a sacred tune.
With every tear, with every sigh,
We find our light beneath the moon.

Upon the winds, the lessons flow,
The heart, a compass, faithful, clear.
With love, all trials help us grow,
Guiding us through shadows near.

In silence deep, we learn to see,
The journey etched in stars above.
In every beat, in every plea,
The language speaks of endless love.

So let us walk in grace divine,
With open hearts and minds set free.
For in this journey, we align,
With all creation's harmony.

Finding Holiness in Every Challenge

In troubled times, a spark appears,
A glimmer of the sacred truth.
With every struggle, shed our tears,
We find His grace within our youth.

Each mountain faced, a lesson learned,
In fires of trial, faith is forged.
For through the pain, a light returns,
In every heart, love is engorged.

When darkness wraps the path we take,
The holy whispers ever near.
In fractured souls, we slowly wake,
To find the light true courage steers.

With every fall, we rise anew,
Holding the truth in feeble hands.
For in His love, we break on through,
Transforming strife into holy strands.

So let us cherish every fight,
For in each challenge, grace we find.
Through trials fierce, we reach the light,
As love unites our weary kind.

Insights Under the Gaze of Stars

Beneath the heavens, dreams unfold,
Each twinkling light a prayer in flight.
Through cosmic dance, the truths are told,
Guiding our hearts into the night.

With every breath, the universe speaks,
In silence deep, we still our minds.
The starlit whispers, wisdom seeks,
Awakens the soul, love unwinds.

In shadows cast by worldly fears,
The stars remind us of our place.
For every tear and joy that nears,
Reflects His love, a gentle grace.

In cosmic tales of olden days,
We find our purpose, ever clear.
With every star, a sacred blaze,
Our hearts aligned to what we hear.

So let us gaze and seek the light,
In night's embrace, we find our way.
For under stars, our souls ignite,
In boundless love, we're led to stay.

Dialogues with the Divine

In quiet moments, hearts converse,
With whispers that the spirit knows.
In prayerful sighs, we break the curse,
Of earthly chains, the love still grows.

Through gentle thoughts, the answers flow,
In every doubt, a spark of light.
For in His arms, we come to know,
That faith ignites the darkest night.

Each word exchanged, a sacred bond,
In stillness, wisdom starts to bloom.
In every pain, He teaches beyond,
And fills our hearts to chase the gloom.

With open eyes, we seek the truth,
In every shout and every sigh.
The dialogues breathe life anew,
As love is written in the sky.

So let us talk in grace and trust,
For in His presence, we're made whole.
With every prayer, a holy gust,
Will guide us on this journey, soul.

Glimpses of the Infinite

In quiet moments, light does gleam,
Reflections of the endless dream.
Above the clouds, the heavens sing,
Whispers of hope that angels bring.

A dance of stars, the night unfolds,
Celestial stories yet untold.
With every breath, the spirit soars,
Connected deep to sacred shores.

Each joy and pain, a step we take,
In search of truth, our hearts awake.
Embrace the vastness of the skies,
In love's embrace, the spirit flies.

Through trials faced, we find our way,
In faith we rise, come what may.
The universe, a wondrous space,
In every heart, divine's embrace.

So let us gaze where beauty lies,
In simple acts, the quiet sighs.
For in the stillness, we may see,
Glimpses of the infinite, free.

Harmony Found in Dissonance

In chaos loud, a truth does dwell,
A symphony that breaks the spell.
In shadows cast by fear and doubt,
A melody emerges, stout.

Each note that clashes, rich and bold,
A tapestry of stories told.
In discord's grasp, we find a tune,
A dance of life beneath the moon.

When rivers crash and mountains sway,
In every storm, the light will play.
In fervent hope, the soul will rise,
A harmony beneath the skies.

Through trials faced, the heart grows wise,
In each challenge, potential lies.
The beauty found in every fall,
Is woven deep within the all.

So let us sing through joy and pain,
Embrace the sun, the gentle rain.
For in dissonance, we are found,
A sacred bond, a holy sound.

The Truths Unraveled by Time

In every tick, the world unfolds,
A tale of dreams, of hearts so bold.
Through seasons past, the future gleams,
In whispered truths and silent dreams.

The sands of time, like rivers flow,
Unraveling paths that we may know.
With every dawn, a chance to see,
The tapestry of history.

We journey forth, with lessons learned,
In every heart, a flame that burns.
With every loss, a gift we gain,
In sorrow's echo, wisdom reigns.

As shadows dance on ancient stone,
The essence of the world is shown.
Oracles in nature's guise,
Reveal the truth that never dies.

So linger not in moments brief,
For in each second lies belief.
Time whispers softly, don't be blind,
Embrace the truths our hearts may find.

Steps on the Path of Enlightenment

With every step, the path unfolds,
In gentle grace, the spirit holds.
Through shadowed woods and light so pure,
The heart, in silence, learns to cure.

In stillness found, the answers wait,
Each moment shared, a sacred state.
The journey bends, the way is long,
In faith and love, we find our song.

With open eyes, the world appears,
A dance of light that calms our fears.
In truth's embrace, the soul takes flight,
The endless quest to seek the light.

From mountain high to valley deep,
The lessons learned, the memories keep.
Through trials faced, we rise anew,
In every heart, the light shines through.

So walk with care, and tread with grace,
Each step a prayer, a holy space.
For on this path, divinity waits,
In every soul, the truth resonates.

Echoes of Eternity

In silence of the night, we pray,
Whispers of love, guiding the way.
Stars above, a celestial choir,
Echoes of faith that lift us higher.

Each dawn anew, mercy descends,
Boundless grace, a hand that mends.
In shadows long, His light will gleam,
Forever held in a sacred dream.

Hearts entwined in a holy dance,
With every step, the heart's romance.
Through trials faced, we stand as one,
Embracing the gift of the risen Son.

In quietude, His voice we hear,
With open hearts, we cast off fear.
In sacred space, our spirits soar,
Echoes of eternity, forevermore.

With every breath, our souls unite,
An endless love, our guiding light.
In faith we move, on this sacred ground,
In echoes of eternity, we are found.

A Tapestry Woven in Trials

In darkest nights, the threads we weave,
A tapestry of hope we conceive.
With every tear, a pattern grows,
In trials faced, His mercy flows.

Each knot binds strength to the heart,
In woven tales, we're never apart.
Through tempests fierce, our spirits rise,
With hands held high, we touch the skies.

From ashes deep, new life will bloom,
In faith we trust, dispelling gloom.
The colors bright, the shadows blend,
In love's embrace, our hearts will mend.

Each thread a prayer, a whispered sigh,
As we journey forth, never shy.
In unity, our voices sing,
A tapestry of grace, forever bringing.

Let trials mold us, shape our fate,
In sacred hands, we resonate.
With gratitude, our hearts will soar,
A tapestry woven, forevermore.

Songs of the Unseen

In the stillness, a song takes flight,
Voices of angels, in the night.
Whispers of love, a gentle breeze,
Songs of the unseen, put hearts at ease.

Through eyes of faith, we hear the call,
In every moment, He guides us all.
In trials faced, His grace bestowed,
Songs of the unseen, as paths are rode.

With hands uplifted, we offer praise,
In sacred moments, we're lost in gaze.
The hymn of hearts, so sweet and clear,
Songs of the unseen, we hold so dear.

In every heartbeat, divine refrain,
A symphony that eases pain.
In faith we rise, in hope we stand,
Songs of the unseen, a guiding hand.

So let us sing through joy and strife,
In every melody, we find our life.
With hearts aglow, our spirits free,
Songs of the unseen, eternally.

Finding Harmony in Chaos

In chaos swirling, peace is found,
In the stillness, grace abounds.
With every storm, we learn to see,
Harmony that sets souls free.

When shadows creep and doubts arise,
Look to the heavens, where hope lies.
In tangled paths, our strength will grow,
Finding harmony in the flow.

Through trials faced, our spirits blend,
In every heartbeat, an unseen friend.
In discordant notes, we hear the song,
Finding harmony where we belong.

With faith as our guide, we make our way,
In darkest nights, we'll find the day.
Through chaos fierce, love lights the road,
Finding harmony in every load.

So let us dance in the tempest's eye,
With open hearts, we'll reach the sky.
In sacred trust, we take our stand,
Finding harmony, hand in hand.

Pilgrim's Note of Life

In the quiet dawn, we tread,
Footsteps soft on sacred ground.
Each breath a prayer, each step a vow,
Awakening the light profound.

The road is long, the heart will yearn,
Wisdom found in every turn.
With faith as guide, we journey on,
In the path of love, we learn.

Through valleys deep and mountains high,
Each tear a testament, each sigh.
In unity, our voices raise,
To honor grace, our souls reply.

The stars above, a map divine,
Leading us to what's truly thine.
In trials faced, we find our way,
A pilgrim's note, a sacred sign.

At journey's end, reflections born,
In love embraced, no soul forlorn.
For every step held purpose true,
In life's great dance, we are reborn.

The Heart's Map to the Sacred

In stillness of the evening hour,
A whisper calls, a gentle power.
The heart knows paths we cannot see,
A guide toward eternity.

Each joy we share, a compass bright,
Each pain a lesson, bringing light.
In love's embrace we chart our course,
Finding peace in the sacred source.

The burdens bore become the bridge,
Unfolding faith, we reach the ridge.
In sacred space, we learn to trust,
The heart's map leads, as love is just.

With every beat, the truth unfolds,
In silent prayer, the spirit holds.
For seeking hearts will surely find,
The sacred calls, the heart aligned.

So let us walk, hand in hand,
In grace we rise, united stand.
For every path adorned with grace,
In the heart's map lies sacred space.

Reflections from the Mountain's Peak

Upon the summit, wisdom waits,
A breath of peace, the soul relates.
The view reveals life's grand design,
In every shadow, light does shine.

Clouds drift by, a fleeting thought,
In silence born, our lessons taught.
With arms open wide to the sky,
We surrender all, the self must die.

Mountains high, where spirits soar,
Remind us what we're journeying for.
In nature's embrace, we find our way,
As hearts align, the mind will sway.

Each stone we pass, a story told,
Of dreams pursued, of hands that hold.
In solitude, the truth we glean,
Reflections show what once had been.

From peaks of trials to valleys low,
In every heartbeat, love will grow.
So climb the heights, face fears anew,
For every summit leads to you.

The Litany of Life's Lessons

In the rhythm of the morning light,
We gather lessons, pure and bright.
In gratitude, our hearts will sing,
The beauty found in simple things.

Each tear we shed, a seed of grace,
In trials faced, we find our place.
With open hands, we learn to give,
In sharing love, we truly live.

The whispers of the past remind,
The journey's rich, the soul refined.
In pain and joy, a balance found,
In every heartbeat, sacred sound.

So let us walk through fire and rain,
Embrace the joy, the love, the pain.
In every lesson, light will grow,
The litany of life, we bestow.

As seasons change and sun descends,
In unity our spirit mends.
With every breath, the lesson clear,
To love and learn, we persevere.

Beyond the Horizon of Understanding

In the stillness of the night, we seek,
Wisdom flows within us, so unique.
Stars above, a guide to our plight,
Beyond the horizon, we find the light.

Questions arise like waves on the sea,
In silence, we ponder, set our spirits free.
Faith holds us steady, fear fades away,
In the depth of our hearts, He leads the way.

Mountains may rise, and valleys may fall,
Yet in His embrace, we rise above all.
Echoes of truth in every heart's song,
Together in grace, we learn to belong.

With every step, we journey anew,
Finding solace in love, pure and true.
Unraveling mysteries, hand in hand,
In the tapestry of life, we take a stand.

So let us wander, ever so bold,
Through realms of the spirit, secrets unfold.
Beyond the horizon, our souls entwined,
In faith and in love, His light we find.

A Pilgrimage Through the Heart.

Upon this path, we venture far,
Guided by the light of a distant star.
With humble steps, we tread the earth,
Finding our purpose, discovering worth.

Through valleys deep and mountains grand,
We carry the promise, hand in hand.
Every heartbeat tells a tale,
In the silence, love will prevail.

The journey is long, the way often steep,
Yet within our spirits, the joy we keep.
In moments of stillness, we hear the call,
United in faith, we shall not fall.

With every sunrise, hope breaks anew,
In the warmth of His presence, we are renewed.
Each prayer a melody, each song a star,
Together in faith, we've come so far.

So let the heart guide, with trust as our light,
Through the shadows, we carry His sight.
A pilgrimage sacred, the soul's true art,
Forever we wander, a journey through heart.

Lessons from the Luminous Path

In the dawn of wisdom, softly we tread,
Seeking the truths that have long been said.
Beneath the shadow, in silence we learn,
From whispers of light, our spirits will yearn.

Each step is a lesson, each stumble a grace,
In the dance of existence, we find our place.
With every heartbeat, the universe sings,
Carving the story that faith surely brings.

The luminous path stretches far and wide,
In the depths of our soul, we take a stride.
Embracing the rhythm, we find our design,
With love as our compass, forever we shine.

In the garden of moments, we blossom and bloom,
Chasing the shadows that once brought us gloom.
Lessons of patience etched in the air,
In the heart of the seeker, hope lingers there.

So let go of doubt, let ambition ignite,
With grace as our guide, we embrace the light.
In faith's gentle hands, our spirits align,
The luminous path, forever divine.

Echoes of the Divine Whisper

In the stillness of prayer, His voice we find,
Whispers of love, gentle and kind.
Through trials and storms, He carries our fears,
With each echo of faith, our vision clears.

Mountains tremble at the sound of His call,
In moments of doubt, He comforts us all.
The heart is a vessel, where grace takes flight,
In the dance of the spirit, we bathe in the light.

Every breath is a promise, sacred and true,
In the echoes of silence, He speaks to me and you.
Guided by love, we walk this great land,
With each step in faith, He holds our hand.

The divine whispers softly through the trees,
In the rustle of leaves, our souls find ease.
With hearts intertwined, we answer the plea,
In the symphony of life, we are set free.

So listen closely to the whispers within,
For in each gentle note, our journey begins.
Echoes of the divine, forever resonate,
In the melody of existence, we celebrate.

Transcendence in the Ordinary

In stillness, we find the grace,
The whispered prayers fill the space.
A cup of water, a shared smile,
In these moments, we see the mile.

Life's tapestry woven tight,
Each mundane task shines bright.
As we bow to the simple things,
In humility, our spirit sings.

The rising sun, a gentle call,
In nature's rhythm, we stand tall.
The dust of earth, the breath of life,
In every heartbeat, joy and strife.

The fragrance of bread, a warm touch,
In the ordinary, we feel so much.
Transcendence found in love's embrace,
Eternal echoes in each space.

So let our hearts learn to believe,
In small wonders, we shall achieve.
The sacred hidden in the light,
Transcendence shines, our guiding sight.

The Divine Canvas of Knowledge

In every leaf, a story told,
Wisdom within, like gems of gold.
Each question asked, a sacred quest,
Unraveling truths, we are blessed.

A tapestry woven with threads of light,
In shadows of doubt, we seek what's right.
The mind's vast ocean, deep and wide,
Navigating waves, where answers reside.

Respect the silence, for there you'll find,
The echoes of ages that shape the mind.
In the dance of thought, divinity roams,
Crafting knowledge in sacred homes.

Each lesson learned, a stepping stone,
In the garden of wisdom, we are never alone.
With open hands and eager heart,
The divine canvas, a living art.

So ponder deeply, and seek what's true,
In the quest for knowledge, find the view.
In the light of insight, shadows fade,
In every thought, God's mark is laid.

The Light Shines Through Cracks

In the brokenness, hope does gleam,
Through tender fractures, we still dream.
A flicker of faith in darkest night,
The light shines through, a beacon bright.

In the cracks of our hearts, love's embrace,
Redemption whispers with gentle grace.
Beneath the weight of sorrow's tale,
A sliver of light can never fail.

Each scar tells of battles fought,
The beauty found in what was sought.
In vulnerability, strength takes root,
From whispered fears, we grow, we shoot.

So let us gather in broken places,
To find the beauty in lost faces.
For even in fragments, hope can bloom,
Casting away the shadows of gloom.

In the soft glow of a spirit unchained,
Resilience grows, the heart unfeigned.
Through every crack, let light arise,
In love's embrace, our spirit flies.

Embracing the Unseen Threads

In the fabric of life, each thread connects,
Invisible ties through time, it reflects.
With gentle hands, we weave our days,
In love's design, our spirit sways.

The silence speaks, where echoes dwell,
In every story, a sacred spell.
From heart to heart, we share our truth,
In whispered hopes, we find our proof.

Each encounter, a sacred dance,
In fleeting moments, we take a chance.
The unseen threads bind us tight,
In the tapestry, day and night.

Embrace the mystery, rise above,
In every thread, the light of love.
In trials faced, we find our way,
Guided by grace, come what may.

So hold each other in this weave,
With open hearts, we learn to believe.
In the unseen threads, our souls entwine,
In love, in hope, forever shine.

Lessons Carved in Time's Clay

In the quiet of dawn, wisdom appears,
Each moment a whisper, calming our fears.
Lessons shaped gently, with patience and care,
Chiseled through trials, with love we declare.

The hands of the maker, guide us in grace,
Molding our spirits, in life's sacred space.
Through shadows and light, our essence refined,
In the heart of the storm, true strength we find.

With faith as our compass, we journey ahead,
Crafting our purpose with hope lightly spread.
In the soil of compassion, our roots intertwine,
Each step a reminder, of love so divine.

Time's fleeting moments, a treasure transformed,
In the tapestry woven, our spirits are warmed.
Each lesson a flower, in the garden of grace,
Blooms in our hearts, as we cherish this place.

So let us be humble, in stillness we learn,
To honor the wisdom, that time will return.
With hands wide open, let us share and embrace,
The lessons of love, in this holy space.

The Unfolding of Sacred Truth

In the silence of being, truth softly sings,
Calling us closer to the love that it brings.
Layers upon layers, the heart shall explore,
In seeking the sacred, we find evermore.

Each question a doorway, each doubt a chance,
To dive into mystery, to awaken our dance.
In shadows and brightness, the path intertwines,
Revealing the sacred, in life's grand designs.

From ages long past, the echoes resound,
In whispers of wisdom, our souls are unbound.
The stories of ancients, in verses are penned,
Teaching us courage, that hope shall transcend.

Through trials and triumphs, the truth lies revealed,
In moments of grace, our hearts are healed.
The unfolding journey, a mirror of light,
Guiding the seeker through the dark of night.

So gather the lessons, with reverence tread,
In the garden of faith, let our spirits be fed.
For the truth we uncover, shall shine ever bright,
In the tapestry of love, we find our true sight.

The Celestial Symphony of Growth

Amidst the vast silence, a melody plays,
Notes of creation, in infinite ways.
Each soul a vessel, of harmony's grace,
Joining the cosmos in this sacred space.

With stars as our audience, we dance and we spin,
Embracing the rhythms that echo within.
Through seasons of change, our spirits shall soar,
In the beauty of growth, we're called to explore.

Each heartbeat a verse in the symphony grand,
Crafted by love's gentle, guiding hand.
From the roots to the branches, all life is a song,
A chorus of nature, where we all belong.

With each passing moment, we blossom and bend,
In unity's song, we discover our blend.
Through trials and laughter, we flourish with zest,
In the light of the heavens, our spirits find rest.

So let us awaken to the music we share,
In the dance of the cosmos, let go of despair.
For in this divine symphony, we're woven so tight,
Together in harmony, we shine with pure light.

Fruits of the Journey

In the garden of life, we sow and we reap,
Miracles blossom from promises we keep.
With faith as our guide, we wander and roam,
Finding the treasures that beckon us home.

Each step on the path, a lesson to glean,
In the tapestry woven, the unseen is seen.
The fruits of our labor, both bitter and sweet,
Nourish the spirit, as we grow from defeat.

The laughter and tears, a blend of the soul,
Every joy and sorrow, part of the whole.
In the rhythm of time, our stories unfold,
Each chapter a treasure, more precious than gold.

From wilderness vast, to the peaks of the light,
We gather the strength, to continue our fight.
The fruits of the journey, a feast from above,
Shared between hearts, as we blossom in love.

So let us remember, the seeds that we sow,
In the garden of kindness, may compassion grow.
For the fruits of our journey, are meant to be shared,
An offering of grace, in a world that has dared.

The Covenant of Experience

In the world of shadows and light,
We walk the path of our days,
With wisdom gained from the fight,
And grace that guides our ways.

Moments woven in divine trust,
Each trial a measure of faith,
In struggles, we learn we must,
Embrace the love in our wraiths.

With every tear that we shed,
A promise blooms in the night,
The whispers of hope like bread,
Feed our souls with pure delight.

Through valleys low and mountains high,
We carry the weight of our quest,
In silence, we lift our hearts high,
Finding peace in every test.

For in the dance of joy and pain,
The covenant is made anew,
In the beauty and the strain,
We find the light that comes through.

Embracing the Divine Mysteries

In the stillness of early dawn,
Where silence cradles the soul,
We seek the truth that moves on,
As shadows embrace the whole.

In the wonder of the unseen,
The sacred whispers take flight,
Each moment a precious sheen,
Reflecting the divine light.

The heart opens through each prayer,
In longing, we find our way,
With every breath, a new layer,
Of faith that guides us each day.

Embracing all thoughts profound,
In the depths of the quiet night,
We gather what we have found,
As we reach for heaven's height.

In the mysteries, we find grace,
A journey shared in the light,
In unity, we find our place,
And together, we take flight.

Threads of Enlightenment

In the tapestry of the skies,
Threads of stories intertwine,
Each moment a blessed surprise,
With divine patterns that shine.

In quietude, the heart learns slow,
To savor each thread of peace,
As wisdom's river starts to flow,
In seeking, our burdens cease.

With every breath, we weave anew,
A fabric of love and hope,
In the colors, the vibrant hue,
We find strength in how we cope.

Our paths may twist, and nights grow long,
Yet the light within stays bright,
Together, we hum a soft song,
In harmony, wrongs turn right.

Threads of insight gently spun,
Looming miracles in the heart,
In the endless dance of the One,
We find solace, a sacred art.

A Prayer for the Weary Spirit

In the stillness of aching night,
We lift our voices in prayer,
Help us rise with renewed might,
Let love and light be our share.

For weary souls that wander lost,
Guide us through the shadowed path,
In trials, may we find our cost,
And turn despair into our laugh.

With trembling hearts, we seek your grace,
In solace, we yearn to abide,
Grant us courage to face each place,
With faith as our constant guide.

Through valleys deep and mountains steep,
Hold us close in warm embrace,
In your arms, our burdens keep,
In your light, we find our space.

A prayer for strength, we humbly send,
To those struggling, near and far,
In togetherness, may we mend,
Our spirits guided by your star.

Sacred Reflections in Still Waters

In still waters, grace does flow,
Mirroring skies where blessings grow.
Quiet whispers in the breeze,
God's gentle touch puts hearts at ease.

The surface calm, a sacred tome,
Where spirits dwell, and souls find home.
Each ripple holds a prayer sincere,
In these depths, His love draws near.

Beneath the surface, life awake,
In every heart, a path to take.
Reflections deep, we seek His light,
Guided gently through the night.

Oft we wander, lost in haste,
Yet in silence, we find our place.
With every breath, a moment sweet,
In still waters, our spirit meets.

So let us gaze, with hearts so pure,
In sacred silence, His voice is sure.
Each drop of water tells His tale,
With faith as a ship, we shall not fail.

The Grace of Growth

In humble soil, the seeds do lie,
Awaiting warmth from the sky.
With gentle rains, they start to rise,
Embracing sun, they touch the skies.

Through struggles faced, the roots go deep,
In the silence, our dreams we keep.
Each bloom a story, rich and bright,
Reflecting love, the purest light.

Seasons change, yet hope remains,
In every joy, in all the pains.
For in our hearts, a seed is sown,
The grace of growth is ever known.

We walk the path with faith in hand,
Together, we shall always stand.
With every step, new life we bring,
A wondrous song of love we sing.

So let our hearts be ever free,
To grow and strive, to seek and see.
In God's embrace, we find our way,
The grace of growth will guide our day.

Pilgrimage of the Heart

On a journey, brave and long,
The heart seeks truth, where it belongs.
Each step we take, a prayer unfurled,
In the pilgrimage of this world.

With every mile, a lesson learned,
In sacred fires, our souls are burned.
The road is rough, yet filled with grace,
In each encounter, we find our place.

Through valleys low and mountains high,
The spirit soars, the heart must fly.
In trust we walk, through night and day,
The light of love will lead the way.

In every tear, a river flows,
To wash our feet, as the journey goes.
Each heartbeat echoes a call so dear,
In the pilgrimage, we draw near.

So let us tread with hearts ablaze,
In every challenge, sing His praise.
For every path, and every part,
Is a sacred quest, a pilgrimage of the heart.

In the Embrace of Sacred Silence

In the stillness, sacred grace,
We find our hearts as we seek His face.
With quietude, our souls can mend,
In sacred silence, we comprehend.

Beneath the noise of worldly strife,
In hushed whispers, we touch true life.
For in the calm, His spirit speaks,
Reviving joy in weary peaks.

Moments pause, where time does cease,
In gentle still, we feel His peace.
With every breath, we draw Him near,
In the embrace, there is no fear.

To listen deep, to ponder wide,
In sacred silence, there's no divide.
Here in this space, our spirits soar,
In love's embrace, we are restored.

So let us bask in quiet grace,
Where every heart finds its rightful place.
In sacred silence, let love reign,
A holy moment, free from pain.